D0883633

Elytes, Ody~~~~~ ~~~~~~~
Viking Press, 1981.
3 3029 00843 3153

CENTRAL

JUL - 1982

**SACRAMENTO PUBLIC LIBRARY**
**SACRAMENTO, CALIFORNIA**

DEMCO

# ODYSSEUS ELYTIS

CHOSEN AND INTRODUCED BY

# Edmund Keeley and Philip Sherrard

TRANSLATED BY
Edmund Keeley, George Savidis,
Philip Sherrard, John Stathatos,
Nanos Valaoritis

# Odysseus Elytis

## SELECTED POEMS

THE VIKING PRESS
NEW YORK

Selection, Introduction and Translations by the Editors
Copyright © 1981 by Edmund Keeley and Philip Sherrard

Translations in Part III copyright © 1981 by John Stathatos
and copyright © 1981 by Nanos Valaoritis

All rights reserved

First published in 1981 by The Viking Press
625 Madison Avenue, New York, N.Y. 10022

Published simultaneously in Canada by
Penguin Books Canada Limited

LIBRARY OF CONGRESS CATALOGING IN PUBLICATION DATA
Elytēs, Odysseas, 1911–
    Odysseus Elytis, selected poems.
    I. Keeley, Edmund.     II. Sherrard, Philip.     III. Title.
PA5610.E43A25     889'.132     81-65282
ISBN 0-670-29246-X                   AACR2


Grateful acknowledgement is made to the following for permission to reprint copyrighted
material:

*The Devin-Adair Company:* "The Isles of Greece" from *Shores of Darkness: Poems and
Essays* by Demetrios Capetanakis, with an Introduction by John Lehmann, 1949.

*Houghton Mifflin Company:* Extracts from *Maria Nefeli* in Nanos Valaoritis's
translation are used by permission of Houghton Mifflin Company, publishers of *Maria
Nephele,* translated by Athan Anagnostopoulos, copyright © 1981 by Odysseus Elytis.

*University of Pittsburgh Press:* Selections from *The Axion Esti* by Odysseus Elytis,
translated by Edmund Keeley and George Savidis. Copyright © 1974 by Edmund Keeley
and George Savidis.


Printed in the United States of America
Set in CRT Electra
Designed by Ann Gold

CENTRAL

c . 1

# CONTENTS

## PART II   1959–1960

## PART III   1971–1979

# INTRODUCTION

The non-Greek world has only slowly, even perhaps grudgingly, come to recognize that modern Greece possesses a flourishing tradition of poetry. Thirty years ago poets like Solomos, Palamas, Cavafy, Sikelianos and Seferis were all but unknown outside Greece, and this in spite of the fact that their work for the most part was completed during the first half of this century and in the case of Solomos well over a hundred years ago. Today this situation has changed, and these poets are beginning to receive the acknowledgement due to them. Translations of their work exist in most major European languages, not least of all in English, and studies of individual writers are becoming increasingly frequent. The fact that in the last two decades the Swedish Academy has awarded the Nobel Prize for Literature to two Greek poets—to George Seferis in 1963 and to Odysseus Elytis, the subject of this present anthology, in 1979—has set the international seal on this greatly overdue recognition.

If one tries to explain why such recognition was withheld for so long, one will probably say in the first instance that it is because so few readers of poetry know the Greek language. This is of course true. But it is only a partial explanation. Equally important is the fact that in the mind of the educated and poetry-reading Westerner, Greece has inevitably been identified with classical Greece, especially in the form attributed to it at the time of the Renaissance. This has meant that Greek poets have been labouring under the shadow of their illustrious forbears, a circumstance that has either concealed them altogether or implied that they could not be recognized unless they conformed to an image that in many ways is totally alien to them. Demetrios Capetanakis, in his essay "The Greeks are Human Beings" published in 1947, was among the first to attempt to point out to Western readers how difficult this made it for the Greek who was trying to be true to his own particular, non-classical genius; and he wrote his short, bitter poem "The Isles of Greece" as a kind of protest against the alien image that the educated Westerner constantly imposed on the contemporary Greek world:

> The sun is not in love with us,
> Nor the corrosive sea;
> Yet both will burn our dried-up flesh
> In deep intimacy
>
> With stubborn tongues of briny death
> And heavy snakes of fire,
> Which writhe and hiss and crack the Greek
> Myth of the singing lyre.

In the Greek world itself, however, Angelos Sikelianos had written long before this of the curtain of aesthetic rationalism that, first issuing from Rome and the Italian Renaissance and then consolidated in the eighteenth century, had made the true face of Greece all but unrecognizable in the West. And more recently, in an interview with Ivar Ivask published in *World Literature Today* in 1975, Elytis too has spoken of how, in order to find this true face, contemporary Greek poets like Seferis and himself have been forced "to destroy the tradition of rationalism which lay heavily on the Western world" and "to regard Greek reality without the prejudices that have reigned since the Renaissance."

What is this sense of Greece's living reality that these poets seek to oppose to the classical stereotype conceived by the Western humanist? First of all, the most immediate roots of the country's poetic heritage are to be found not in the ancient world but in the demotic tradition, which has shaped modern Greece's language and which, stemming from the Byzantine world, has found rich expression in the literature of seventeenth-century Crete (above all in the long epic poem *Erotokritos*), as well as in folk song and ballad. Alongside this demotic tradition—sometimes informing it and sometimes repulsed by it—is the great liturgical tradition of the Greek Orthodox Church, with its own more complex poetic forms and a language that harks back to the Greek of the ancient world even more than it looks forward to spoken demotic Greek. But behind these two direct "literary" sources of modern Greek poetry lies the physical and metaphysical presence of the Greek world itself: its seas, its skies, its great mountain ranges, its dusty fig trees and its coruscating olive trees, its ancient monuments, its harsh, penumbral islands, its explosive light, its proud, tormented people, all not yet entirely violated by the grosser obscenities of tourism and commerce.

It is this world that Elytis celebrates in his early poems, those that appeared in his first two volumes, *Orientations* (1940) and *Sun the First* (1943). The reader will be aware at once of the surrealist element in these poems. This of course is not accidental, though it is easy to make too much of it. Elytis, who had read deeply in the works of the French surrealists during his formative years in the Thirties, regarded surrealism as a weapon in his struggle to liberate the image of Greece from the straitjacket of Western rationalism. "Surrealism," he notes, "with its antirationalistic character, helped us to make a sort of revolution by perceiving the Greek truth. At the same time, surrealism contained a supernatural element, and this enabled us to form a kind of alphabet out of purely Greek elements with which to express ourselves." In other words, for Elytis surrealism had two functions, both positive. First, it provided a way of escape from the domination of a merely rational approach to things; and second, it made it possible to affirm in these things—in the "purely Greek elements"—a numinous or mystical presence both within and beyond their direct physical appearance. It is the awareness of what one might call the metaphysical dimension of the physical world of Greece that allows Elytis to transcend that dualism between the world of the senses and the supernatural world implicit in much so-called "nature poetry." It allows him, as he puts it, to elevate the world of the senses "to a level that is sacred." This he achieves through the metamorphosis of the world of the senses in the light of the supernatural world. Such a metamorphosis not only resolves apparent dissonances but also makes it possible for one element in the poet's inner and outer landscape to become another—a morning's mood a tree, summer a naked youth, a girl an orange—without contradiction, without this change being merely a surrealist device calculated to produce a startling effect. Elytis's poetry is not "pagan," if by that term one means that it exalts the physical world simply in its own right. On the contrary, this poetry's intense, even ecstatic lyricism is the result of the poet's capacity to perceive the sacred aspect of visible things, and to give these things a kind of luminous transparency in which they can interpenetrate or metamorphose without thereby losing their identity. This perception, so vividly expressed in Elytis's early poetry, pervades all his work and perhaps more than anything else gives it its unity.

Elytis's first two volumes appeared during the Second World War, in which he himself served early as an officer in the heroic Albanian Campaign that resisted the Italian invasion of Greece. It was inevitable that these years, during which Greece suffered more than her share of foreign military occupation, mass killings, starvation and much else, should have had a profound effect on the poet. His first attempt to assimilate and give significance to this new depth of experience in his poetry resulted in his *Heroic and Elegiac Song for the Lost Second Lieutenant of the Albanian Campaign*, published in 1945. Already in this poem the emphasis has shifted away from the purely celebratory to focus on the apparently tragic dilemma of man who, in a world essentially good, is yet caught in the crossfire of evil and pays with his life for his defence of what he regards as justice. But it is with *The Axion Esti*, published in 1959, that Elytis makes what is perhaps his most ambitious attempt to fuse his lyrical ecstatic sense of things with a more sombre, reflective, and even philosophical assessment of his own country's—and by implication mankind's—destiny in historical and traditional terms.

This attempt required, in the first place, a more elaborate and complex formal structure than is evident in his earlier poems. The model for this Elytis found above all in the liturgical tradition of the Greek Orthodox Church. It also required a far more conscious use of images and symbols derived from the major phases of Greek tradition than had Elytis's earlier work. In his early work, Elytis had deliberately avoided too much reliance on classical imagery and myth because of the artificial role they were assigned in the post-Renaissance literature of Europe. "I have never employed ancient myths in the usual manner," he remarks in the Ivask interview previously cited; and he continues: "No doubt it is advantageous for a Greek poet to employ ancient myths, because he thus becomes more accessible to foreign readers. . . . I have reacted against this, often quite consciously, because I thought it was a bit too facile. . . . Since my chief interest was to find the *sources* of the neo-Hellenic world, I kept the mechanism of myth-making but not the figures of mythology." In *The Axion Esti*, however, and especially in the stanzas from "The Gloria" included here, the ancient gods and their habitations, even the mythical figures in Homer, not only hover in the background but actually appear overtly, made to seem quite at home in the poem's contemporary setting.

Even so, as is evident from the middle section, "The Passion," it is the non-classical sources that are still dominant in *The Axion Esti*: the Greek Orthodox liturgy, the folk songs, Dionysios Solomos and other nineteenth-century demotic writers. The two prose poems called "First Reading" and "Second Reading" (pages 52, 54) are especially effective in dramatizing this link with the post-classical tradition, beginning with the liturgical analogy suggested by their titles and the biblical echoes that follow in the text. But kinship between past and present is conveyed most forcefully by the poet's deliberate invocation of the style and verisimilitude of the *Memoirs* of General Makriyannis, a simple man of the people who rose to be one of the leaders in the Greek War of Independence in 1821. This beautifully honest, down-to-earth prose document is written in a version of nineteenth-century demotic and in script that George Seferis described as being "like an old wall in which, if one looks closely, one can trace every movement of the builder, how he fitted one stone to the next, how he adjusted every effort he made to what had gone before and was to follow after, leaving on the finished building the imprint of the adventures of an uninterrupted human action." The two "Readings" are chapters in Elytis's own "memoirs" of the Albanian Campaign, and this account of his emotionally complex personal experiences is brilliantly served by his adaptation of Makriyannis's colourful and forthright style.

Perhaps the best example of Elytis's subtle merging of the Greek past with a more accessible present is "The Autopsy" (page 66), from the 1960 volume *Six and One Pangs of Conscience for the Sky*. Here we are given a portrait of what the poet finds to be most vital in his contemporary landscape through the metaphor of a body cut open to reveal its concealed mysteries. First, it is the body of the poet that is the subject of the autopsy, and what the probing knife uncovers are those sources in the modern world that have best nourished his poetry. But as is usual in Elytis's verse from any period, the figure of the poet cannot be separated from its roots in his native soil, so that we come to see the dissected body of this poem as that of his country as well; and what the autopsy serves to reveal is the timeless synthesis of features that gives Greece what Elytis sees as her true face. The mythical dimension emerges with the reader's growing awareness that this autopsy is also meant to suggest a kind of ritual sacrifice preparing the way for perennial fertility in keeping with ancient tradition, specifically that which offers us the resurrected Adonis and the prospect that "we shall have early fruit this year."

During the past decade Elytis has published prolifically, as our selection in the final part of this anthology makes clear. Though the focus of his poems has remained essentially as he described it early in his career—namely, to create a personal mythology that correlates his response to the world around him and his metaphysical perception—he has continued to experiment with new modes for expressing his perennial themes. His latest volume, for example, links in its title, *Maria Nefeli*, a girl's name and the region of clouds, and it shapes its statement through the *en face* juxtaposition of a young girl's liberated "leap into ideas" and a much older persona's attempt to understand and define her free-wheeling vision in his own more traditional terms. These later works have consolidated Elytis's status in his own country, where he is now regarded as continuing the tradition formed by poets like Solomos, Sikelianos and Seferis. Yet despite the international recognition that came to him with his Nobel Prize, translations of his poetry, especially into English, have been relatively few and scattered. We hope that this volume, limited though it necessarily is, will help to communicate to a wider audience something of what he has achieved over the past forty-five years.

E.K.
P.S.
*Katounia, Limni, Evia*
*Summer 1980*

# I
1940-1945

FROM ORIENTATIONS
(1940) ❧❧❧❧❧❧❧❧❧❧❧❧❧❧❧❧❧❧❧

TRANSLATED BY
Edmund Keeley and Philip Sherrard

# AEGEAN

Love
The network of islands
And the prow of its foam
And the gulls of its dreams
On its highest mast a sailor
Whistles a song.

Love
Its song
And the horizons of its voyage
And the sound of its longing
On its wettest rock the bride
Waits for a ship.

Love
Its ship
And the nonchalance of its winds
And the jib sail of its hope
On the lightest of its waves an island
Cradles the arrival.

II

Playthings, the waters
In their shadowy flow
Speak with their kisses about the dawn
That begins
Horizoning—

And the pigeons in their cave
Rustle their wings
Blue awakening in the source
Of day
Sun—

The northwest wind bestows the sail
To the sea
The hair's caress
In the insouciance of its dream
Dew-cool—

Waves in the light
Revive the eyes
Where life sails towards
The recognition
Life—


III

The surf a kiss on its caressed sand—Love
The gull bestows its blue liberty
To the horizon
Waves come and go
Foamy answer in the shell's ear.

Who carried away the blonde and sunburnt girl?
The sea-breeze with its transparent breath
Tilts dream's sail
Far out
Love murmurs its promise—Surf

## SEVEN NOCTURNALS•

### I

Dream after dream arrived
For the jasmine's birthday,
Night after night for the white insomnia
Of the swans

Coolness is born among leaves
As is the starlit sensation
In boundless sky.

### II

Propitious starlight brought on silence
And behind the silence an intrusive melody
Lover,
Temptress of sounds from another country.

 Now the dying shadow remains
And its cracked confidence,
Its incurable dizziness—there.

### III

All the cypress trees point toward midnight
All the fingers
Toward silence

Outside the dream's open window
Slowly, slowly
The confession unwinds
And, as pure colour, deviates toward the stars!

### IV

A shoulder fully bared
Like truth

6

Pays for its precision
At this edge of evening
Which shines in isolation
Under the secret half-moon
Of my nostalgia.


V

Unguarded night was taken by memories
Dark blue
Red
Yellow

Its open arms filled with sleep
Its rested hair with wind
Its eyes with silence.


VI

Unfathomable night, bitterness without limit
Sleepless eyelash
Pain burns before it turns to sobbing
Loss leans off-balance before its weighing

Ambush at the point of death
When thought is broken by the useless meandering design
On the apron of its destiny.


VII

The moon's diadem on the brow of night
When shadows divide up the surface
Of vision

And pain measured by the practised ear
Unintentionally collapses
Inside an idea made worthless by the melancholy
Of evening's bugle-call.

7

# ANNIVERSARY

I brought my life this far
To this spot which struggles
Forever near the sea
Youth upon the rocks, breast
To breast against the wind
Where is a man to go
Who is nothing other than a man
Reckoning with the coolness his green
Moments, with waters the visions
Of his hearing, with wings his remorse
O Life
Of a child who becomes a man
Forever near the sea when the sun
Teaches him to breathe there where the shadow
Of a seagull vanishes.

I brought my life this far
White addition, black total
A few trees and a few
Wet pebbles
Gentle fingers to caress a forehead
What forehead
Anticipation wept all night and is no more
Nor is anyone.
Would that a free footstep be heard
A rested voice rise
The poops ripple at the jetty, inscribing
A name in darker blue upon their horizon
A few years, a few waves
Sensitive rowing
In the bays surrounding love.

I brought my life this far
Bitter furrow in the sand that will vanish
—Whoever saw two eyes touch his silence
And mixed with their sunshine, closing a thousand worlds
Let him remind his blood in other suns

Nearer the light
There is a smile that pays for the flame—
But here in this ignorant landscape that loses itself
In an open and merciless sea
Success sheds
Whirling feathers
And moments that have become attached to the earth
Hard earth under the soles of impatient feet
Earth made for vertigo
A dead volcano.

I brought my life this far
A stone pledged to the liquid element
Beyond the islands
Lower than the waves
Next to the anchors
—When keels pass, splitting with passion
Some new obstacle, and triumph over it
And hope dawns with all its dolphins
The sun's gain in a human heart—
The nets of doubt draw in
A figure in salt
Carved with effort
Indifferent, white,
Which turns toward the sea the void of its eyes
Supporting infinity.

## HELEN

Summer was killed with the first drop of rain
Words that had given birth to starlight were drenched
All those words whose single goal was You.
Where will we stretch our hands now the weather no longer takes us into
    account?
On what will we rest our eyes now the distant horizons have been
    shipwrecked by the clouds
Now your eyelashes have closed over our landscapes
And—as though the fog passed through us—
We are left alone, utterly alone, encircled by your dead images?

Forehead to windowpane we keep watch for the new sorrow
Death will not lay us low so long as You exist
So long as there exists a wind elsewhere to enjoy you fully
To clothe you from close by as our hope clothes you from far away
So long as there exists elsewhere
A green plain reaching beyond your laughter to the sun
Telling the sun secretly how we will meet again
No, it isn't death we will confront
But the tiniest autumnal raindrop
An obscure feeling
The smell of wet earth in our souls that grow continually farther apart.

And if your hand is not in our hand
If our blood is not in the veins of your dreams,
The light in the immaculate sky
And the unseen music inside us
Still bind us, sad wayfarer, to the world
It is the damp wind, the autumnal hour, the separation,
The elbow's bitter prop on the memory
That awakens when night starts to cut us off from the light
Behind the square window facing toward grief
Revealing nothing
Because it has already become unseen music, flame in the fireplace, chime
    of the huge clock on the wall
Because it has already become
A poem, line succeeding line, sound keeping pace with the rain, tears and
    words—
Words not like others but these too with a single goal: You.

# ADOLESCENCE OF DAY

Adolescence of day, joy's springhead
The ancient myrtle waves its banner
The breast of the larks will open to the light
And a song will hang suspended in mid-air
Sowing the four winds
With golden grains of fire

Liberating earth's beauty.

# ODE TO SANTORINI

You came out of the thunder's belly
Shuddering in the penitential clouds
Bitter stone, tested, defiant
You summoned the sun to be your first witness
To confront with you the impetuous radiance
To open out with a crusading echo in the sea

Sea-woken, defiant,
You thrust up a breast of rock
Scored with the south wind's inspiration
For pain to engrave its guts there
For hope to engrave its guts there
With fire, lava, smoke
With words that convert the infinite
You gave birth to the voice of day
You raised,
To the green and rose porticos of vision,
The bells struck by the exalted intellect
Praising the birds in the mid-August light.

Close to the wave's thud, to the foam's lament,
Among the eucharists of sleep
When night wandered through the wilderness of stars
Searching for the testimony of dawn
You experienced the joy of birth

You were the first to leap forth into the world,
Porphyrogenite, sea-begotten,
You sent to the far horizons
Blessings nurtured in the sea's vigils
To caress the hair of daylight's waking hour.

Queen of the heartbeats, and wings of the Aegean,
With words that convert the infinite
With fire, lava, smoke,
You discovered the great lines of your destiny.

Now justice stands revealed before you
Black mountains sail in the brightness
Longings dig their craters
In the heart's tormented land
And from hope's struggle a new earth is made ready
So that on a morning full of iridescence
The race that vivifies dreams
The race that sings in the sun's embrace
May stride forth with eagles and banners.

O daughter of the highest wrath
Sea-begotten, naked,
Open the glorious gates of man
So that health may sweeten the land
The senses may flower in a thousand colours
Their wings spread wide
So that freedom may blow from all directions.

In the wind's proclamation flash out
The new, the eternal beauty
When the three-hour-old sun rises up
Entirely blue to play the harmonium of creation.

## MARINA OF THE ROCKS •

You have a taste of tempest on your lips—But where did you wander
All day long in the hard reverie of stone and sea?
An eagle-bearing wind stripped the hills
Stripped your longing to the bone
And the pupils of your eyes received the message of chimera
Spotting memory with foam!
Where is the familiar slope of short September
On the red earth where you played, looking down
At the broad rows of the other girls
The corners where your friends left armfuls of rosemary.

But where did you wander
All night long in the hard reverie of stone and sea?
I told you to count in the naked water its luminous days
On your back to rejoice in the dawn of things
Or again to wander on yellow plains
With a clover of light on your breast, iambic heroine.

You have a taste of tempest on your lips
And a dress red as blood
Deep in the gold of summer
And the perfume of hyacinths—But where did you wander
Descending toward the shores, the pebbled bays?

There was cold salty seaweed there
But deeper a human feeling that bled
And you opened your arms in astonishment naming it
Climbing lightly to the clearness of the depths
Where your own starfish shone.

Listen. Speech is the prudence of the aged
And time is a passionate sculptor of men
And the sun stands over it, a beast of hope
And you, closer to it, embrace a love
With a bitter taste of tempest on your lips.

It is not for you, blue to the bone, to think of another summer,
For the rivers to change their bed
And take you back to their mother
For you to kiss other cherry trees
Or ride on the northwest wind.

Propped on the rocks, without yesterday or tomorrow,
Facing the dangers of the rocks with a hurricane hairstyle
You will say farewell to the riddle that is yours.

# THE AGE OF BLUE MEMORY

Olive trees and vineyards far as the sea
Red fishing boats beyond, far as memory
August's golden sheaves in midday slumber
With seaweed and shells. And that green boat,
Just launched, still blessing the water's peaceful breast with "God will
    provide"

The years went by, leaves or pebbles,
I recall the young men, the sailors who left,
Their sails dyed the colour of their hearts
Their songs telling of the four horizons
And the north winds tattooed on their chests

What was I looking for when you arrived, painted by the rising sun
The sea's age in your eyes
The sun's health in your body—what was I looking for
Deep in the sea-caves, the spacious dreams
Where the wind scattered its feelings like foam
Unknown and blue, carving his sea-emblem on my chest

Sand on my fingers, I closed my fingers
Sand on my eyes, I clasped my fingers
It was the sorrow—
I remember it was April when I first felt your human weight
Your human body, clay and sin,
Like our first day on earth
Feast-day of the amaryllis—I remember your pain
It was a deep bite on the lips
A deep nail-mark on the skin where time's track is traced eternally

I left you then
And a deafening wind shook the white houses
Shook white feelings freshly washed into the sky
Radiant with a smile

Now I will have beside me a pitcher of deathless water,
I will have a diagram of the wind's shattering freedom
And those hands of yours where Love will be tormented
And that shell of yours where the Aegean will echo.

# AEGEAN MELANCHOLY

What linking of soul to the halcyons of the afternoon!
What calm in the voices of the distant shore!
The cuckoo in the trees' mantilla,
And the mystic hour of the fishermen's supper,
And the sea playing on its concertina
The long lament of the woman,
The lovely woman who bared her breasts
When memory found the cradles
And lilac sprinkled the sunset with fire!

With caïque and the Virgin's sails
Sped by the winds they are gone,
Lovers of the lilies' exile;
But how night here attends on sleep
With murmuring hair on shining throats
Or on the great white shores;
And how with Orion's gold sword
Is scattered and spilled aloft
Dust from the dreams of girls
Scented with mint and basil!

At the crossroad where the ancient sorceress stood
Burning the winds with dry thyme, there,
Lightly, holding a pitcher full with the waters of silence,
Easily, as though they were entering Paradise,
Supple shadows stepped . . .
And from the crickets' prayer that fermented the fields
Lovely girls with the moon's skin have risen
To dance on the midnight threshing floor . . .

O signs, you who pass in the depths
Of the mirror-holding water—
Seven small lilies that sparkle—
When Orion's sword returns
It will find poor bread under the lamp
But life in the star's embers;
It will find generous hands linked in space,

Abandoned seaweed, the shore's last children,
Years, green gems . . .

O green gem—what storm-prophet saw you
Halting the light at the birth of day,
The light at the birth of the two eyes of the world!

# FORM OF BOEOTIA

Here where the lonely glance blows over stone and aloe
Here where time's steps sound deeply
Where huge clouds unfurl their golden banners
Above the sky's metope,
Tell me from what source eternity sprung
Tell me which is the sign you care for
And what is the helminth's fate


O land of Boeotia made shining by the wind


What became of the chorus of naked hands under the palaces
Of mercy that rose like sacred smoke
Where are the gateways with the ancient singing birds
And the uproar waking the people's terror
When the sun entered as though triumphant
When fate writhed on the heart's spear
And fratricidal twittering caught fire
What became of the deathless libations of March
Of the Greek lines in the waters of greenery


Foreheads and elbows have been wounded
Time, in an abundance of sky, has rolled vermilion
Men have forged ahead
Full of pain and dreaming


Acrid form! Ennobled by the wind
Of a summer storm that leaves its white-hot tracks
In the lines of hills and eagles
In the lines of destiny on your palm


What can you confront, what can you wear
Dressed in the music of grass, and how do you move on
Through the heather or sage
To the arrow's final point

On this red Boeotian soil
In the rocks' desolate march
You will light the golden sheaves of fire,
Uproot memory's evil fruitfulness,
Leave a bitter soul to the wild mint.

# THE MAD POMEGRANATE TREE•

*Inquisitive matinal high spirits*
à perdre haleine

In these all-white courtyards where the south wind blows
Whistling through vaulted arcades, tell me, is it the mad pomegranate tree
That leaps in the light, scattering its fruitful laughter
With windy wilfulness and whispering, tell me, is it the mad
    pomegranate tree
That quivers with foliage newly born at dawn
Raising high its colours in a shiver of triumph?

On plains where the naked girls awake,
When they harvest clover with their light brown arms
Roaming round the borders of their dreams—tell me, is it the mad
    pomegranate tree,
Unsuspecting, that puts the lights in their verdant baskets
That floods their names with the singing of birds—tell me
Is it the mad pomegranate tree that combats the cloudy skies of the
    world?

On the day that it adorns itself in jealousy with seven kinds of feathers,
Girding the eternal sun with a thousand blinding prisms
Tell me, is it the mad pomegranate tree
That seizes on the run a horse's mane of a hundred lashes,
Never sad and never grumbling—tell me, is it the mad pomegranate tree
That cries out the new hope now dawning?
Tell me, is that the mad pomegranate tree waving in the distance,
Fluttering a handkerchief of leaves of cool flame,
A sea near birth with a thousand ships and more,
With waves that a thousand times and more set out and go
To unscented shores—tell me, is it the mad pomegranate tree
That creaks the rigging aloft in the lucid air?

High as can be, with the blue bunch of grapes that flares and celebrates
Arrogant, full of danger—tell me, is it the mad pomegranate tree
That shatters with light the demon's tempests in the middle of the world
That spreads far as can be the saffron ruffle of day

Richly embroidered with scattered songs—tell me, is it the mad
    pomegranate tree
That hastily unfastens the silk apparel of day?

In petticoats of April first and cicadas of the feast of mid-August
Tell me, that which plays, that which rages, that which can entice
Shaking out of threats their evil black darkness
Spilling in the sun's embrace intoxicating birds
Tell me, that which opens its wings on the breast of things
On the breast of our deepest dreams, is that the mad pomegranate tree?

# FROM SUN THE FIRST
## (1943) ❧❧❧❧❧❧❧❧❧❧❧❧❧❧❧❧❧❧❧

TRANSLATED BY
Edmund Keeley and Philip Sherrard

## "I NO LONGER KNOW THE NIGHT . . ."

I no longer know the night, death's terrible anonymity
A fleet of stars has dropped anchor in the depths of my soul
Hesperus, sentinel, so that you may shine
Close to the heavenly breeze of an island that dreams of me
Announcing the dawn from its high crags
My two eyes enfolding you steer you by the star
Of my true heart: I no longer know the night

I no longer know the names of the world that denies me
With clarity I read the shells, the leaves, the stars
Vain is my antagonism on the sky's highroads
Unless it is the dream that gazes at me again
With tears as I cross the sea of deathlessness
Hesperus, beneath the arc of your golden fire
The night that is only night I now no longer know.

# BODY OF SUMMER

A long time has passed since the last rain was heard
Above the ants and lizards
Now the sun burns endlessly
The fruit paints its mouth
The pores in the earth open slowly
And beside the water that drips in syllables
A huge plant gazes into the eye of the sun.

Who is he that lies on the shores beyond
Stretched on his back, smoking silver-burnt olive leaves?
Cicadas grow warm in his ears
Ants are at work on his chest
Lizards slide in the grass of his armpits
And over the seaweed of his feet a wave rolls lightly
Sent by the little siren that sang:

"O body of summer, naked, burnt
Eaten away by oil and salt
Body of rock and shudder of the heart
Great ruffling wind in the osier hair
Breath of basil above the curly pubic mound
Full of stars and pine needles
Body, deep vessel of the day!

"Soft rains come, violent hail
The land passes lashed in the claws of a snow-storm
Which darkens in the depths with furious waves
The hills plunge into the dense udders of the clouds
And yet behind all this you laugh carefree
And find your deathless moment again
As the sun finds you again on the sandy shores
As the sky finds you again in your naked health."

## "BURNISHED DAY,
## CONCH OF THE VOICE . . ."

Burnished day, conch of the voice that fashioned me
Naked, to step through my perpetual Sundays
Between the shores' cries of welcome,
Let your wind, known for the first time, blow freely
Unfold a lawn of tenderness
Where the sun can roll his head
Can enflame the poppies with his kiss
Poppies nourished by men so fine
That the sole mark on their bare chests
Is the blood of defiance that annuls sorrow
And attains the remembrance of liberty.

I spoke of love, of the rose's health, of the ray
That by itself goes straight to the heart,
Of Greece that steps so surely on the sea
Greece that carries me always
Among naked snow-crowned mountains.

I give my hand to justice
Diaphanous fountain, sublimest spring,
My sky is deep and changeless
All I love is incessantly reborn
All I love is always at its beginning.

## "DRINKING THE SUN OF CORINTH . . ."

Drinking the sun of Corinth
Reading the marble ruins
Striding across vineyards and seas
Sighting along the harpoon
A votive fish that slips away
I found the leaves that the sun's psalm memorizes
The living land that passion joys in opening.

I drink water, cut fruit,
Thrust my hand into the wind's foliage
The lemon trees water the summer pollen
The green birds tear my dreams
I leave with a glance
A wide glance in which the world is recreated
Beautiful from the beginning to the dimensions of the heart!

## "I LIVED THE BELOVED NAME..."

I lived the beloved name
In the shade of the aged olive tree
In the roaring of the lifelong sea

Those who stoned me live no longer
With their stones I built a fountain
To its brink green girls come
Their lips descend from the dawn
Their hair unwinds far into the future

Swallows come, infants of the wind
They drink, they fly, so that life goes on
The threat of the dream becomes a dream
Pain rounds the good cape
No voice is lost in the breast of the sky

O deathless sea, tell me what you are whispering
I reach your morning mouth early
On the peak where your love appears
I see the will of the night spilling stars
The will of the day nipping the earth's shoots

I saw a thousand wild lilies on the meadows of life
A thousand children in the true wind
Beautiful strong children who breathe out kindness
And know how to gaze at the deep horizons
When music raises the islands

I carved the beloved name
In the shade of the aged olive tree
In the roaring of the lifelong sea.

## "THIS WIND THAT LOITERS . . ."

This wind that loiters among the quinces
This insect that sucks the vines
This stone that the scorpion wears next to his skin
And these sheaves on the threshing floor
That play the giant to small barefoot children.

The images of the Resurrection
On walls that the pine trees scratched with their fingers
This whitewash that carries the noonday on its back
And the cicadas, the cicadas in the ears of the trees.

Great summer of chalk
Great summer of cork
The red sails slanting in gusts of wind
On the sea-floor white creatures, sponges
Accordions of the rocks
Perch from the fingers even of bad fishermen
Proud reefs on the fishing lines of the sun.

No one will tell our fate, and that is that.
We ourselves will tell the sun's fate, and that is that.

## "ALL DAY LONG WE WALKED
## IN THE FIELDS . . ."

All day long we walked in the fields
With our women, suns, and dogs
We played, sang, drank water
Fresh as it sprang from the ages

In the afternoon we sat for a moment
And we looked deeply into each other's eyes
A butterfly flew from our hearts
It was whiter
Than the small white branch at the tip of our dreams
We knew that it was never to disappear
That it did not remember at all what worms it bore

At night we lit a fire
And round about it sang:

Fire, lovely fire, do not pity the logs
Fire, lovely fire, do not turn to ash
Fire, lovely fire, burn us
                    tell us of life.

We tell of life, we take it by the hands
We look into its eyes and it returns our look
And if this which makes us drunk is a magnet, we know it
And if this which gives us pain is bad, we have felt it

We tell of life, we go ahead
And say farewell to its birds, which are migrating

We are of a good generation.

## "WITH WHAT STONES, WHAT BLOOD, AND WHAT IRON . . ."

With what stones, what blood, and what iron,
With what fire are we made
Though we seem pure mist
And they stone us and say
That we walk with our heads in the clouds
How we pass our days and nights
God only knows

My friend, when night wakens your electric grief
I see the tree of the heart spreading
Your arms open beneath a pure Idea
To which you call
But which will not descend
For years and years:
It up there, and you down here

And yet longing's vision awakens flesh one day
And there where only bare solitude once shone
A city now laughs lovely as you would have it
You almost see it, it is waiting for you
Give me your hand so that we may go there before the Dawn
Floods it with cries of triumph
Give me your hand—before birds gather
On the shoulders of men to announce in song
That Virginal Hope is seen coming at last
Out of the distant sea.

We will go together, and let them stone us
And let them say we walk with our heads in the clouds—
Those who have never felt, my friend,
With what iron, what stones, what blood, what fire,
We build, dream, and sing.

# HEROIC AND ELEGIAC SONG FOR THE LOST SECOND LIEUTENANT OF THE ALBANIAN CAMPAIGN

(1945) 🌱🌱🌱🌱🌱🌱🌱🌱🌱🌱🌱🌱🌱🌱🌱🌱🌱🌱🌱

TRANSLATED BY
Edmund Keeley and Philip Sherrard

There where the sun first dwelt
Where time opened like a virgin's eyes
As the wind snowed flakes of almond blossom
And horsemen lit up the tips of the grass

There where the hoof of a gallant plane tree beat
And high up a banner waved to earth and water
Where no back ever bent under a gun's weight
But all the sky's labour,
All the world, shone like a waterdrop
In early morning, at the mountain's foot

Now, as though God were sighing, a shadow lengthens

Now agony stoops and with bony hands
Plucks and crushes the flowers one by one;
In gullies where the water has stopped flowing
Songs die from the dearth of joy;
Rocks like monks with chill hair
Cut the bread of wilderness in silence.

Winter penetrates to the mind. Something evil
Will strike. Hair of the horse-mountain bristles.

High overhead vultures share out the sky's crumbs.


II

Now in the turbid water an agitation rises

Wind clinging to foliage
Vomits its dust
Fruits spit out their seeds
Earth hides her stones
Fear digs a tunnel and burrows headlong
When from the sky's thicket
A she-wolf cloud, howling,

Scatters a storm of shudders over the plain's skin
And then the snow spreads, spreads, the merciless snow
And then it goes snuffling into the hungry valleys
And then drives men to answer:
Fire or the knife!

For those who have set out with fire or the knife
Evil will strike here. The cross need not despair
Only let the violets pray a long way from it.


III

For those men night was a more bitter day
They melted iron, chewed the earth
Their God smelled of gunpowder and mule-hide

Each thunderclap was a death riding the sky
Each thunderclap a man smiling in the face
Of death—let fate say what she will.

Suddenly the moment misfired and struck courage
Hurled splinters head-on into the sun
Binoculars, sights, mortars, froze with terror.

Easily, like calico that the wind rips
Easily, like lungs that stones have punctured
The helmet rolled to the left side . . .

For one moment only roots shook in the soil
Then the smoke dissolved and the day tried timidly
To beguile the infernal tumult.

But night rose up like a spurned viper
Death paused one second on the brink—
Then struck deeply with his pallid claws.


IV

Now with a still wind in his quiet hair
A twig of forgetfulness at his left ear

He lies on the scorched cape
Like a garden the birds have suddenly deserted
Like a song gagged in the darkness
Like an angel's watch that has stopped
Eyelashes barely whispered goodbye
And bewilderment became rigid . . .

He lies on the scorched cape
Black ages round him
Bay at the terrible silence with dog's skeletons
And hours that have once more turned into stone pigeons
Listen attentively.
But laughter is burnt, earth has grown deaf,
No one heard that last, that final cry
The whole world emptied with that very last cry.

Beneath the five cedars
Without other candles
He lies on the scorched cape.
The helmet is empty, the blood full of dirt,
At his side the arm half shot away
And between the eyebrows—
Small bitter spring, fingerprint of fate
Small bitter red-black spring
Spring where memory freezes.

O do not look O do not look at the place where life
Where life has left him. Do not say
Do not say how the smoke of dream has risen
This is the way one moment this is the way
This is the way one moment deserts the other
And this is the way the all-powerful sun suddenly deserts the world.


V

Sun, were you not all-powerful?
Bird, were you not joy's unresting moment?
Brightness, were you not the cloud's audacity?
And you, garden, were you not an odeum of flowers
And were you not, dark root, flute of the magnolia.

As a tree quivers in the rain
As the empty body is blackened by fate
As a madman lashes himself with snow
And two eyes give way to tears—
Why, asks the eagle, where is the young man?
And all the eaglets wonder where the young man is.
Why, asks the mother, sighing, where is my son?
And all mothers wonder where her child is.
Why, asks the friend, where is my brother?
And all his friends wonder where the youngest of them is.
They touch snow and the fever burns
They touch a hand and it freezes
They bite into bread and it drips blood
They gaze deeply into the sky and it turns livid
Why why why why does death not give warmth
Why such unholy bread
Why a sky like that, there where the sun used to live.


VI

He was a fine young man. The day he was born
The mountains of Thrace bent down to show
The wheat rejoicing on the land's shoulders.
The mountains of Thrace bent down to spit
First on his head, then on his chest, then into his tears.
Greeks with formidable arms appeared
And raised him in swaddling-bands of the north . . .
Then days sped by, they hurled stones in sport
Gambolled astride fillies.
Then the early Strymons rolled down
Till gypsy anemones everywhere rang their bells
And from earth's confines came
Sea-shepherds driving flocks of seal
To where a cave breathed deeply
To where a huge rock sighed.

He was a strong young man.
Nights lying with girls of the orange grove
He stained the stars' great raiment,

The love inside him was such
That he drank all the earth's taste in wine,
Then danced with the white brides
Till dawn heard and spilt light into his hair,
Dawn that with open arms found him
Scratching the sun in the saddle of two small branches,
Painting the flowers,
Or with tenderness lulling
The small sleepless owls . . .
Ah, what strong thyme his breath,
What a proud map his naked chest
Where freedom, where the sea resounded . . .

He was a brave young man.
With his gold buttons and his pistol
With a man's air in his stride
And his helmet a shining target
(his brain, that had never known evil,
was penetrated so easily)
With his soldiers on his right and left
And the avenging of injustice in front of him
—Fire against lawless fire!—
With the blood above his eyebrows
The mountains of Albania thundered
Then they melted snow to wash
His body, dawn's silent shipwreck
And his hands, open spaces of solitude
The mountains of Albania thundered
They did not weep
Why should they weep?
He was a brave young man.


VII

The trees are charcoal that night does not enkindle.
The wind pounces, beats its breast, the wind beats its breast again:
Nothing. In the frost the mountains kneel
Searching for shelter. And, howling, the abyss

Ascends the precipices, from the skulls of the dead . . .
Not even sorrow weeps any more. Like a madwoman
Made childless she goes round and round, a sprig-like cross on her breast
She does not weep. Only, girdled with the black mountains of Epiros,
She rises aloft and sets up a lunar plaque
Lest the planets should see their shadow as they circle
Should hide their rays
And come to a halt
Gasping in chaos dementedly . . .

The wind pounces, beats its breast, the wind beats its breast again
Solitude clasps her black shawl tight
Bent behind month-like clouds she listens
To what does she listen, distant cloud-like months?

With rags of hair on her shoulders—ah, leave her alone—
Half candle half fire a mother weeps—leave her alone—
Leave her to the frozen empty rooms in which she circles.
For fate is no one's widow
And mothers are born to weep, men to struggle
Gardens to flower on a young girl's breast
Blood is to be spilt, surf to thud
And freedom to flash out unceasingly.


VIII

Now that his fatherland has darkened on earth
Tell the sun to find another route
If he wants to save his pride.
Or with soil and water
Let him cast a small sister Greece in blue elsewhere.
Tell the sun to find another route
So as not to confront even a single daisy
Tell the daisy to flower with a new virginity
So that she will not be sullied by alien fingers.

Release the wild pigeons from the fingers
And let no sound speak of the water's suffering

As the sky blows softly into an empty shell
Send no signal of despair to any place
But bring from the gardens of chivalry
Roses where his soul stirred
Roses where his breath played
On a small nymphic chrysalis
That changes its dress as often as satin its sheen
In the sun, as the may-bugs grow drunk on gold-dust
And birds fly swiftly to learn from the trees
Through what seed's germination this famous world was born.


IX

Bring new hands, for now who will ascend
To sing lullabies to the stars' children.
Bring new limbs, for now who will be the first
To join in the dance of the angels.
New eyes—O my God—for now
Who will stoop to the lilies of the beloved.
New blood, for with what joyful greeting will they take fire
And mouth, fresh mouth of bronze and amaranth
For now who will bid the clouds goodbye.

Day, who will confront the peachleaves
Night, who will tame the wheatfields
Who will scatter green candles over the plains
Or cry out courageously in the face of the sun
To clothe himself in storms astride the invulnerable horse
To become the Achilles of the shipyards.
Who will go to the mythical black island
To kiss the pebbles
And who will sleep
To pass through the gulfs of dream
To find new hands, limbs, eyes
Blood and speech
To stand again on the marble threshing floors
And with his holiness grapple—ah, this time—
Grapple with Death.

X

Sun, bronze voice, and holy etesian wind
Swore on his breast to give him life
There was no room for any darker strength
Only with light spilt from the laurel branch
And silver from dew, only there the cross
Flashed, as magnanimity dawned
And kindness, sword in hand, rose up
To proclaim through his eyes and their banners "I live."

Your health, old river, you who see at dawn
Such a child of God, a twig of pomegranate
Between his teeth, perfuming himself in your waters;
Your health, village medlar tree, you who preen yourself
When Androutsos tries to steal his dreams;
And yours, noonday spring, you who touched his feet
And yours too, girl, you who were his Helen,
His little bird, his Holy Virgin, his Pleiades,
Because if only once in a lifetime
Love of a human being were to reverberate, igniting
Star after star, the secret firmaments,
The divine voice would reign always everywhere
Adorning the woods with the tiny hearts of birds
Adorning poets' words with lyres of jasmine.

And let it harrow hidden evil wherever it is to be found—
Let it harrow with fire hidden evil wherever it is to be found.

XI

Those who committed evil—because affliction
Had stolen their eyes—are floundering
Because fear
Had stolen their affliction they are lost in the black cloud
Back, and no longer with plumes on their forehead
Back, no longer with nails on their feet
Where sea strips vine and volcano,

To fields of the homeland again, with the moon for a plough,
To the rocks of the homeland again, with the mandolin of Zalongo,
Back, to where greyhound fingers
Smell flesh and where the tempest lasts
As long as white jasmine in the harvest-time of woman.

Those who committed evil have been taken up by a black cloud
Behind them they had no life of fir tree and cool waters
Of lamb, wine and rifles, rods and vine-trellis
They had no grandfather of oak and angry wind
Standing watch for eighteen days and nights
With bitter eyes.
A black cloud has taken them up—behind them
They had no swashbuckler uncle, no gunloading father,
No mother who has slaughtered with her own hands
Or mother's mother who, breast naked, dancing,
Gave herself to Death's freedom.

Those who committed evil have been taken up by a black cloud
But he who faced it on the sky's highroads
Ascends now alone and glorious.


    XII

With dawn step on the spreading green
He ascends alone and glorious.

Hermaphroditic flowers salute him secretly
And with soft voices that fade into the air they speak to him
Love-sick trees bend towards him
With nests sunk in their armpits
And their branches dipped in the sun's oil
Miracle—what a miracle—down on earth
White tribes with blue ploughshares engrave the fields
Peaks shine in the background
And, deeper still, the inaccessible dreams of spring mountains.

He ascends alone and glorious.
So drenched in light that his heart shows

42

The true Olympus shows through the clouds
And the air is filled with the praise of friends . . .
Now dream beats swifter than blood
Animals congregate at the edge of the path
Grunt and gaze as though they were speaking
The whole world is truly a huge giant
Who cherishes his children.

In the distance crystal bells ring out
Tomorrow, they say, tomorrow: Easter of Heaven.


XIII

In the distance crystal bells ring out

They speak of him who was burnt in life
As a bee in the thyme's ferment;
Of dawn choked in earthen breasts
Though it promised a brilliant day;
Of the snowflake that flashed in the mind and went out
When a distant shot was heard
And high overhead the Albanian partridge flew away lamenting.

They speak of him who had no time even to weep
For the deep sadness of the love of life
He had when the wind grew strong in the distance
And birds croaked on the beams of a ruined mill
For women who drank wild music
Standing at the window clasping their kerchiefs tightly
For women who drove despair to despair
Waiting for a black signal at the meadow's edge.
Then clanging horseshoes beyond the threshold
Speak of his warm, unfondled head
Of his large eyes where life had penetrated
So deeply that it could never come out again.


XIV

Now dream beats swifter in the blood
The world's truest moment signals:

Freedom,
Greeks in the darkness point the way:
FREEDOM
For you the sun will weep for joy.

Rainbow-coloured headlands fall into the water
Ships under full sail cruise among the meadows
The most innocent girls
Run naked in the sight of men
And modesty behind the barrier cries
Friends, no land is more lovely . . .

The world's truest moment signals.

With dawn step on the spreading green
He ascends higher and higher;
Now around him shine
Longings that once were lost
In the loneliness of sin;
Incandescent are his heart's longings;
Birds greet him, they seem to be his brothers
Men call to him, they seem to be his companions
"Birds, blessed birds, death ends here."
"Friends, my dearest friends, life begins here."
A halo of heavenly radiance glitters in his hair

In the distance crystal bells ring out:
Tomorrow, tomorrow, tomorrow: Easter of God.

# II
## 1959-1960

FROM THE AXION ESTI
(1959) ❦ ❦ ❦ ❦ ❦ ❦ ❦ ❦ ❦ ❦ ❦ ❦ ❦ ❦ ❦ ❦ ❦ ❦ ❦ ❦ ❦

TRANSLATED BY
Edmund Keeley and George Savidis

## From THE GENESIS

IN THE BEGINNING the light And the first hour
                        when lips still in clay
                        try out the things of the world
   Green blood and bulbs golden in the earth
   And the sea, so exquisite in her sleep, spread
   unbleached gauze of sky
   under the carob trees and the great upright palms
                      There alone I faced
                      the world
                      wailing loudly
*My soul called out for a Signalman and Herald*
                      I remember seeing then
                      the three Black Women
   raising their arms toward the East
   Their backs gilded, and the cloud they were leaving behind
   slowly fading
                      to the right And plants of other shapes
   It was the sun, its axis in me
   many-rayed, whole, that was calling And
the One I really was, the One of many centuries ago
the One still verdant in the midst of fire, the One still tied to heaven
                      I could feel coming to bend
                      over my cradle
And his voice, like memory become the present,
assumed the voice of the trees, of the waves:
                      "Your commandment," he said, "is this world
                      and it is written in your entrails
                      Read and strive
                      and fight" he said
"Each to his own weapons" he said
And he spread his hands as would
a young novice God creating pain and mirth together
   First the Seven Axes, wrenched with force,
   pried loose from high up in the battlements,
   fell to the ground
                      as in the great Storm
                      at its zero point

                    where a bird gives forth its fragrance
                    from the beginning again
the blood was homing clean
and the monsters were taking on a human shape
                         *So very manifest, the Incomprehensible*
     Then all the winds of my family arrived too
     the boys with puffed-out cheeks
     and tails green and broad, mermaidlike
                         and others, old men: familiar, ancient
                         shell-skinned, bearded
     And they parted the cloud in two, and these again into four
     and what little remained they blew away, chasing it off to the North
     With  broad  foot  and  proudly,  the  great  Tower  trod  the  waters
The line of the horizon flashed
so visible, so dense and impenetrable
                         THIS the first hymn.

BUT BEFORE hearing the wind or music
as I was setting out to find a vista
(climbing a boundless red sand dune
erasing History with my heel)
    I wrestled with my bed sheets What I was looking for was this,
    innocent and tremulous like a vineyard
    deep and unscarred like the sky's other face,
*A drop of soul amidst the clay*

Then he spoke and the sea was born
And I gazed upon it and marvelled
In its centre he sowed little worlds in my image and likeness:

Horses of stone with manes erect
and tranquil amphorae
and slanting backs of dolphins

    Ios, Sikinos, Serifos, Milos
"Each word a swallow
to bring you spring in the midst of summer" he said
And ample the olive trees
    to sift the light through their fingers
    that it may spread gently over your sleep
and ample the cicadas
    which you will feel no more
    than you feel the pulse inside your wrist
but scarce the water
    so that you hold it a God and understand the meaning of its voice
and the tree alone
    no flock beneath it
    so that you take it for a friend
    and know its precious name
sparse the earth beneath your feet
    so that you have no room to spread your roots
    and keep reaching down in depth
and broad the sky above
    so that you read the infinite on your own


THIS WORLD
this small world the great!

50

# From THE PASSION

II

GREEK the language they gave me;
poor the house on Homer's shores.
　　My only care my language on Homer's shores.
There bream and perch
　　windbeaten verbs,
green sea currents in the blue,
　　all I saw light up in my entrails,
sponges, jellyfish
　　with the first words of the Sirens,
rosy shells with the first black shivers.
　　My only care my language with the first black shivers.
There pomegranates, quinces,
　　swarthy gods, uncles and cousins
emptying oil into giant jars;
　　and breaths from the ravine fragrant
with osier and terebinth
　　broom and ginger root
with the first chirping of finches,
　　sweet psalms with the very first Glory Be to Thee.
My only care my language with the very first Glory Be to Thee!
　　There laurel and palm leaves
censer and incense
　　blessing the swords and muskets.
On soil spread with vine-scarves,
　　the smell of roasting lamb, Easter eggs cracking,
and "Christ is Risen,"
　　with the first salvoes of the Greeks.
Secret loves with the first words of the Hymn.
　　My only care my language with the first words of the Hymn!

## THE MARCH TOWARD THE FRONT

AT DAYLIGHT on St. John's, the day after Epiphany, we got our orders to move up to the front again, out there where you don't find weekdays or holidays. We were to take over the line the Artans had been holding till then, from Khimara to Tepeleni. The reason being they'd been fighting since the first day, without a break, and only about half of them were left and they couldn't take it any longer.

Twelve whole days we'd been back there, in the villages. And just as our ears were again getting used to the sweet creaking of the earth and just as we'd begun gingerly to make sense out of a dog's barking or the clang of a distant church bell, they tell us we have to go back to the only sound we really knew: the slow and heavy cannon, the dry and quick machineguns.

Night after night we trudged ahead without stopping, one behind the other, like the blind—sweating to pull our feet out of the mud, sometimes in it up to our knees. Because it was usually drizzling out there on the road, just as it was inside us. And the few times we'd pull up for a rest, not a word, everyone serious and silent, we'd share our raisins one by one under the light from a bit of pine kindling. Or sometimes, when we got the chance, we'd rip off our gear and scratch ourselves wildly until we drew blood. Because the lice were up to our ears, and that was even harder to take than being tired. Finally, through the darkness you'd hear a whistle signalling us to move out, and we'd push off again like pack animals to gain ground before daylight, when we'd make an open target for the planes. Because God didn't know about targets and things, so he'd stick to his habit of making the light come up at the same time every day.

Then, hidden in the ravines, we'd lay our heads down on the heavy side, the one that doesn't give out dreams. And the birds would get mad at us, thinking we weren't taking their talk seriously—and maybe also because we were disfiguring nature for no reason. We were farmers of a different kind, carrying picks and tools of a different kind, damn them.

Twelve whole days back there in the villages we'd gazed for hours on end at the shape of our faces in the mirror. And just as our eyes were getting used again to the old familiar features, and just as we'd begun gingerly to make sense of the bare upper lip or the sleep-filled cheek, they tell us we have to move, so that by the second night we began to feel we were changing again, more so by the third, until on the last, the fourth, it was clear we were no longer the same. Except it seemed we were marching along like a gang made up of all generations and ages, some from now and some from ancient times, turned white by too much beard. Scowling mountain chieftains with their headbands, tough priests, sergeants from the wars of '97 and '12, grim pioneers swinging their axes, Byzantine border guards with their maces and shields still covered with the blood of Turks and Bulgars. Together, no one speaking, groaning on side by side numberless years, crossing mountain ridges and the gorges between, no thought about anything else. Because just as people who get the bad breaks again and again become used to Evil and end up changing its name to Destiny or Fate, so we kept heading straight ahead for what we called the Plague, as we might have said the Fog or the Cloud—sweating to pull our feet out of the mud, sometimes in it up to our knees. Because it was usually drizzling out there on the road, just as it was inside us.

That we were very near the place where you don't find weekdays or holidays, sick people or healthy people, poor or rich, we now knew. Because the roar ahead, like a storm beyond the mountains, kept growing, so that in the end we could clearly read the slow and heavy cannon, the dry and quick machineguns. Also because more and more we started coming across the slow procession of the wounded, heading out the other way. And the medics, with the red cross on their arm bands, would set their stretchers down and spit on their hands, eyes wild for a cigarette. And when they'd hear where we were going, they'd shake their heads and start their tales of blood and terror. But we, the only thing we listened to were those other voices rising in the darkness, still scalding from the fire and brimstone of the depths. "Oi, oi, mana mou," "Oi, oi, mana mou." And sometimes, less often, the sound of stifled breathing, like a snore, and those who knew said that was the rattle of death.

Sometimes they dragged along with them prisoners captured a few hours before in surprise raids by our patrols. Their breath stank of wine and their pockets were full of canned goods or chocolates. But we had nothing, the bridges cut off behind us and our few mules helpless in the snow and the slippery muck.

Finally the moment came when we saw smoke rising here and there in the distance, and along the horizon the first bright red flares.

# THE MULE DRIVERS

IN THOSE DAYS, at long last, after three full weeks, the first mule driv-
ers reached our territory. And they told us a lot about the towns they'd
passed through—Délvino, Saints Saránda, Koritsá. And they unloaded
their salt herring and biscuits with an eye to finishing up as soon as possi-
ble and taking off. Because they weren't used to this booming from the
mountains, it scared them, and so did the black beards on our wasted
faces.

And it happened then that one of them had some old newspapers on
him. And all of us read with amazement—though we'd heard rumours
about it already—how they were celebrating in the capital and how people
in the streets would carry on their shoulders those fighting men back on
leave from their offices in Prevesa and Arta. And the bells would ring the
day long, and in the evening at the theatres they would sing songs and act
out our lives on stage for the crowd to applaud.

Heavy silence fell among us, because our souls had turned fierce from
so many months in the wilderness, and, without saying so, we'd become
very tight about what years we had left. In fact at one point Sergeant Zois,
tears welling in his eyes, brushed aside the rags with news of the world,
giving it the five-fingered sign. And the rest of us didn't say a thing, except
that our eyes showed him something like gratitude.

Then Lefteris, who was standing off by himself rolling a cigarette sto-
ically, as though carrying the helplessness of the universe on his shoulders,
turned to say: "Sergeant, what's the point of fuming about it? Those who
are ordained for herring and biscuits will always go back to herring and bis-
cuits. And the same goes for those with their endless paperwork, and for
those who make their soft beds but don't control them. But let me tell you
one thing: only he who wrestles with the darkness inside him will find his
own place in the sun someday." Then Zois: "So you think I don't have a
wife and fields and troubles of my own, sitting here on watch in the wil-
derness?" And Lefteris answered: "The things one doesn't love, Sarge, are
the things to fear, because they're lost already, no matter how much you
try to cling to them. But there's no way you can lose the things of the
heart, don't you worry, and that's what the wilderness works for. Sooner or
later, those who are meant to find them will find them." Then Zois asked
again: "So who in your opinion is going to find them?" Then Lefteris,

slowly, pointing his finger: "You and I, brother, and anybody else chosen by the moment that's listening to us."

And right then we heard, whistling dark in the air, the shell about to reach us. And we all hit the dirt and lay there face down on the brambles, because by now we knew the markings of the Invisible by heart, and our ears could spot in advance exactly where the fire would open the earth and spill out. And the fire didn't hurt a thing, only a few of the mules reared up on their hind legs and some others scattered in their fright. And as the smoke settled you could see the men who'd led them up there with so much trouble chasing after them with wild gestures. And their faces pale, they went on unloading the herring and biscuits with an eye to finishing up as soon as possible and taking off, because they weren't used to this booming from the mountains, it scared them, and so did the black beards on our wasted faces.

d

*A* SOLITARY SWALLOW *and a costly spring,*
*For the sun to turn it takes a job of work,*
*It takes a thousand dead sweating at the Wheels,*
*It takes the living also giving up their blood.*

*God my Master Builder, You built me into the mountains,*
*God my Master Builder, You enclosed me in the sea!*

*Magicians carried off the body of May,*
*They buried the body in a tomb of the sea,*
*They sealed it up in a deep well,*
*Its scent fills the darkness and all the Abyss.*

*God my Master Builder, You too among the Easter lilacs,*
*God my Master Builder, You felt the scent of Resurrection!*

*Wriggling like sperm in a dark womb,*
*The terrible insect of memory breaks through the earth*
*And bites the light like a hungry spider,*
*Making the shores glow and the sea radiant.*

*God my Master Builder, You girded me with seashores,*
*God my Master Builder, You founded me on mountains.*

e

WITH THE STAR'S LAMP I *went out in the heavens.*
*How, in the frost of the meadows, the world's only shore,*
*Can I find my soul, the four-leaf tear!*

*Weeping myrtle, silvered with sleep,*
*Sprinkled my face. I blow and go alone.*
*How can I find my soul, the four-leaf tear!*

*Leader of rays and magus of bedrooms,*
*Vagabond who knows the future, speak to me.*
*How can I find my soul, the four-leaf tear!*

*My girls are in mourning for the ages,*
*My boys carry guns yet do not know*
*How I can find my soul, the four-leaf tear!*

*Nights with a hundred hands stir my entrails*
*Throughout the firmament. This pain burns.*
*How can I find my soul, the four-leaf tear!*

*With the star's lamp I roam the heavens.*
*In the frost of the meadows, the world's only shore,*
*How can I find my soul, the four-leaf tear!*

## k

*I WILL TONSURE my head, monk of things verdant,*
*And reverently serve the order of birds,*
*I will come to the matins of Fig Trees out of the night,*
*Dew-covered, to bring in my apron*
*Blue, pink, purple*
*And to kindle the generous water drops,*
*I the more generous.*

*I will have for icons the immaculate girls*
*Dressed only in the linen of the open sea,*
*I will pray that my purity assume*
*The myrtle's instinct and the muscle of wild animals,*
*To drown forever in my vigorous entrails*
*The mean, the perverse, the nebulous,*
*I the more vigorous.*

*There will be times of much iniquity,*
*Of profit and honour, of remorse and flogging,*
*The maddened Bucephalus of blood will charge*
*To trample my white yearning,*
*Valour, love, light,*
*And smelling them out as mighty, to neigh,*
*He the more mighty.*

*But then, at the sixth hour of the erect lilies,*
*When my judgement will make a crack in Time,*
*The eleventh Commandment will emerge from my eyes:*
*Either this world or none other shall be*
*The Labour of Birth, the Union with God, the Forever,*
*Which in the justice of my soul I will have proclaimed,*
*I the more just.*

## From THE GLORIA

PRAISED BE the wooden table
the blond wine with the sun's stain
  the water doodling across the ceiling
the philodendron on duty in the corner


  The walls hand in hand with the waves
a foot that gathered wisdom in the sand
  a cicada that convinced a thousand others
conscience radiant like a summer


  PRAISED BE the heatwave hatching
the beautiful boulders under the bridge
  the shit of children with its green flies
a sea boiling and no end to it


  The sixteen deckhands hauling the net
the restless seagull slowly cruising
  stray voices out of the wilderness
a shadow's crossing through the wall


  THE ISLANDS with all their minium and lampblack
the islands with the vertebra of some Zeus

the islands with their boat yards so deserted
the islands with their drinkable blue volcanoes

Facing the meltemi with jib close-hauled
Riding the southwester on a reach
    the full length of them covered with foam
with dark blue pebbles and heliotropes

*Sifnos, Amorgos, Alonnisos*
*Thasos, Ithaka, Santorini*
*Kos, Ios, Sikinos*

PRAISED BE Myrto standing
on the stone parapet facing the sea
    like a beautiful eight or a clay pitcher
holding a straw hat in her hand

The white and porous middle of day
the down of sleep lightly ascending
    the faded gold inside the arcades
and the red horse breaking free

Hera of the tree's ancient trunk
the vast laurel grove, the light-devouring
    a house like an anchor down in the depths
and Kyra-Penelope twisting her spindle

The straits for birds from the opposite shore

a citron from which the sky spilled out

the blue hearing half under the sea

the long-shadowed whispering of nymphs and maples


PRAISED BE, on the remembrance day

of the holy martyrs Cyricus and Julitta,

a miracle burning threshing floors in the heavens

priests and birds chanting the *Ave*:


HAIL Girl Burning and hail Girl Verdant

Hail Girl Unrepenting, with the prow's sword


Hail you who walk and the footprints vanish

Hail you who wake and the miracles are born


Hail O Wild One of the depths' paradise

Hail O Holy One of the islands' wilderness


Hail Mother of Dreams, Girl of the Open Seas

Hail O Anchor-bearer, Girl of the Five Stars


Hail you of the flowing hair, gilding the wind

Hail you of the lovely voice, tamer of demons

Hail you who ordain the Monthly Ritual of the Gardens

Hail you who fasten the Serpent's belt of stars.


Hail O Girl of the just and modest sword

Hail O Girl prophetic and daedalic

# SIX AND ONE PANGS OF
# CONSCIENCE FOR THE SKY
# (1960)

TRANSLATED BY
Edmund Keeley and Philip Sherrard

# BEAUTY AND THE ILLITERATE

Often, at the Dormition of Twilight, her soul took on a certain lightness
from the mountains opposite, though the day had been cruel and to-
morrow was unknown.

Yet, when darkness came and the hand of the priest appeared over the
garden of the dead, She,

Alone, Erect, with the few familiar companions of night—the rosemary
breeze and the charcoal smoke from chimneys—lay awake on the
threshold of the sea

Singularly beautiful.

Words half-formed of waves or half-guessed in a rustling, and others seem-
ingly of the dead, words startled among the cypresses, like strange
Zodiacs circling her head, suddenly illumined her. And an

Unbelievable clarity allowed the true landscape to appear at a great depth
within her,

Where, beside the river, black men fought the Angel, showing in what
manner Beauty is born.

Or what in other terms we call tears.

And as long as her thought lasted, you felt that it overflowed her shining
face, with the bitterness in the eyes and the cheekbones—like those
of an ancient temple servant—enormous

Stretching from the tip of Canis Major to the tip of Virgo.

"And I, far from the pestilence of the city, imagined a desert at her side,
where tears would have no meaning and where the only light would
be that of the fire which devoured all my possessions

"The two of us shoulder to shoulder would sustain the weight of the fu-
ture, sworn to utter silence and to a condominion of the stars

"As though I did not know, illiterate as I am, that it is exactly there, in utter silence, where the most appalling noises are heard

"And that loneliness, from the time it became unendurable to the heart of man, has scattered and sown stars!"

# THE AUTOPSY

And so they found that the gold of the olive root had dripped in the recesses of his heart.

And from the many times that he had lain awake by candlelight waiting for the dawn, a strange heat had seized his entrails.

A little below the skin, the blue line of the horizon sharply painted. And ample traces of blue throughout his blood.

The cries of birds which he had come to memorize in hours of great loneliness apparently spilled out all at once, so that it was impossible for the knife to enter deeply.

Probably the intention sufficed for the evil

Which he met—it is obvious—in the terrifying posture of the innocent. His eyes open, proud, the whole forest moving still on the unblemished retina

Nothing in the brain but a dead echo of the sky.

Only in the hollow of his left ear some light fine sand, as though in a shell. Which means that often he had walked by the sea alone with the pain of love and the roar of the wind.

As for those particles of fire on his groin, they show that he moved time hours ahead whenever he embraced a woman.

We shall have early fruit this year.

# THE SLEEP OF THE BRAVE

They still smell of incense, and their faces are burnt by their crossing through the Great Dark Places.

There where they were suddenly flung by the Immovable

Face-down, on ground whose smallest anemone would suffice to turn the air of Hades bitter

(One arm outstretched, as though straining to be grasped by the future, the other arm under the desolate head, turned on its side,

As though to see for the last time, in the eyes of a disembowelled horse, the heap of smoking ruins)—

There time released them. One wing, the redder of the two, covered the world, while the other, delicate, already moved through space,

No wrinkle or pang of conscience, but at a great depth

The old immemorial blood that began painfully to etch, in the sky's blackness,

A new sun, not yet ripe,

That couldn't manage to dislodge the hoarfrost of lambs from live clover, but, before even casting a ray, could divine the oracles of Erebus . . .

And from the beginning, Valleys, Mountains, Trees, Rivers,

A creation made of vindicated feelings now shone, identical and reversed, there for them to cross now, with the Executioner inside them put to death,

Villagers of the limitless blue:

Neither twelve o'clock striking in the depths nor the voice of the pole falling from the heights retracted their footsteps.

They read the world greedily with eyes now open forever, there where they were suddenly flung by the Immovable,

Face-down, and where the vultures fell upon them violently to enjoy the clay of their guts and their blood.

# LACONIC

Longing for death so scorched me that my brightness returned to the sun.

Who now sends me into the perfect syntax of stone and air,

So he whom I sought, I am.

O flaxen summer, discreet autumn,

Most humble winter,

Life contributes its mite, the leaf of the olive tree,

And in the night of stupidities with a small cricket again vindicates the claim of the Unexpected.

## THE ORIGIN OF LANDSCAPE
## OR THE END OF MERCY

Suddenly the swallow's shadow reaped the glances of its nostalgia: Noon.

With a sharp flint, slowly, skilfully, the sun engraved the wings of the west wind above the shoulders of the Daughter of Justice.

Light working on my flesh, the violet mark appeared for a moment on my chest just where remorse had touched me and I ran madly. Then sleep among steep leaves desiccated me and I was left alone. Alone.

I envied the waterdrop that, unperceived, glorified the lentisk. Would that I could be like that in the miraculous eye privileged to see the end of Mercy.

Or was I perhaps like that? In the harshness of the rock, uncleft from peak to base, I recognized my obstinate jaw. In another age it tore the beast to pieces.

And the sand beyond, settled by the delight the sea once gave me when men blasphemed and I opened my arms wide in my hurry to find solace within her. Was it this I was looking for? Purity?

Water reversing its current, I entered the spirit of the myrtle where lovers take refuge from persecution. Again I heard the silk brushing the hairs of my chest as it panted. And the sound, "my darling", at night, in the ravine where I cut the stars' last moorings and the nightingale was trying to take shape.

Truly, what yearnings and what derision I had to pass through, with a fragment of an oath in my two eyes and my fingers free from corruption. Yes, they were like that, the years when I was struggling to make the endless azure sky so tender.

I spoke. And, turning my face, I again confronted it in the light as it gazed steadfastly at me. Merciless.

It was purity.

Beautiful, and pensive from the shadow of years, under the sun's sema-
phore the Daughter of Justice wept

As she watched me walking once more through this world, without gods,
but weighed down with what I had snatched from death while still
living.

Suddenly the swallow's shadow reaped the glances of its nostalgia: Noon.

# THE OTHER NOAH

I threw the horizons into lime, and with slow but steady hand, set out to consecrate the four walls of my future.

It is time, I said, for lust to begin its priestly mission and in a Cloister of Light to secure that transcendent moment when the wind scraped a bit of cloud over the highest tree on earth.

Those things I struggled to find on my own in order to preserve my style in the face of contempt, those things will now arrive—from the strong acid of the eucalyptus to a woman's rustling—to be saved in the Ark of my asceticism.

Also the farthest, most bypassed stream; and among the birds, the only one they left me, the sparrow; and from the scanty vocabulary of bitterness, two, at most three words: bread, longing, love.

(O Times, you who warped the rainbow and tore the crumb from the sparrow's beak and didn't leave even the tiniest voice of clear water to spell out my love in green places,

I who tearlessly endured the orphanage of brilliant light, O Times, I do not forgive you.)

And when, devouring each other's guts, men begin to diminish, and from one generation to the next,

Evil rolling on, become enraged in the abandoned sky,

The white particles of my isolation, whirling above the corrosion of a ruined world, will move to justify my small understanding,

And, gathered together again, will open the horizons in the distance, will crunch one by one the bitter words on the water's lips,

Offering the old meaning of my despair.

Like a bite from the leaf of a heavenly eucalyptus, may the holy day of sensuality give out its odour

And may Woman, Bearer of Green Things, climb the current of Time
   naked

And slowly, royally, opening her fingers, once and for all release the bird

Over mankind's unholy weariness, so that from the place where God erred,
   now may fall

The trillings of Paradise!

# SEVEN DAYS FOR ETERNITY

SUNDAY.—Morning, in the Temple of the Calfbearer. I declare: may lovely Myrto become as true as a tree; and may her lamb, gazing for one moment straight into the eyes of my assassin, punish the most bitter of futures.

MONDAY.—Presence of grass and water at my feet. Which means that I exist. Before or after the glance that will turn me to stone, I raise my right hand, holding high a huge blue ear of wheat. To establish a new Zodiac.

TUESDAY.—Exodus of the numbers. Battle between 1 and 9 on a deserted shore full of black pebbles, heaps of seaweed, with gigantic vertebrae of beasts on the rocks.
My two beloved old horses neighing as they stand above the steam rising from the sea's sulphur.

WEDNESDAY.—On the other side of the thunderbolt. The burnt hand that will flower again. To smooth out the folds of the world.

THURSDAY.—Open door: stone steps, geranium heads, and beyond, transparent roofs, paper kites, flakes of shell in the sun. A goat slowly ruminates the ages, and the smoke, peaceful, rises between his horns.
The moment when, in the back courtyard, the gardener's daughter is kissed secretly, and from her extreme delight a flowerpot falls and breaks open.
O, if I could only preserve that sound!

FRIDAY.—"Feast of the Transfiguration" of the women I have loved without hope. Echo: Ma-ri-naa! E-le-niii! With each stroke of the bell, lilac falls into my arms. Then strange light, and two quite dissimilar pigeons carry me high into a large house covered with ivy.

SATURDAY.—Cypress tree of my kin cut by taciturn cruel men: for betrothal or death. They dig the earth round about and sprinkle it with carnation water.
Even though I've already uttered the words that demagnetize the infinite.

74

# III
## 1971-1979

Translations in this section
are by John Stathatos and Nanos Valaoritis,
as indicated by their initials

# DEATH AND RESURRECTION OF CONSTANTINE PALAIOLOGOS (1971)

I

As he stood there erect before the Gate and armoured in his sorrow

Far from the world which his soul strove to reckon by the span of Paradise And much harder than stone for he'd never been looked at tenderly—sometimes his crooked teeth gleamed strangely white

And as he passed with eyes focused a little above people's stature and picked out One of them who smiled at him the True One whom death could never touch

He was careful to pronounce the word *sea* clearly so that all the dolphins within it gleamed And the wilderness vast enough for God and each and every drop rising steadily to the sun

As a child he had seen the gold braid on adult shoulders blaze and vanish And one night he remembers how during a great storm the ocean's maw groaned and it clouded and yet did not consent to wait

To live this life is hard, yet worth it for a little pride.

II

What now my God Now that he had to strive with thousands as well as his own loneliness he he who with just one word could slake the whole world's thirst

What if they'd taken all from him His cross-gartered sandals and his sharp trident and the castle wall which he bestrode each day holding the reins against the wind like a fractious and playful sailboat

And a sprig of verbena      rubbed on a girl's cheek      at midnight
      to kiss her      (how the moon's waters rippled over the stone steps
three flights above the sea . . . )

Noontide of night      And not a soul alongside him      Only his faithful words running their colours all together to place a spear of white light in his hand

And opposite      along the whole length of the walls      heads set like ants in plaster as far as the eye could see

"Noontide of night—life's but a flash!"      he cried and rushed into the fray      dragging an endless golden line behind him

And felt at once      from a great distance      the deadly pallor taking him.


                III

Now      as the sun's shuttlecock spun ever faster      the courts dipped into winter and emerged again dyed red by the geraniums

And the little cool domes like blue medusas reached ever higher each time towards the silver which the wind filigraned for the depiction of other times      more distant

Maidens      their embrace lighting a summer daybreak      brought him fresh laurel leaves and from the deeps myrtle branches still dripping iodine

While underneath his feet he heard      engulfed in the great sewer
      prows of black ships      the ancient blackened wood      from whence      wild-eyed Virgins still standing called reproachfully

Horses sprawled upon the earth banks      the ruined buildings great and small      turmoil and dust swirling in the air

With one unyielding word always between his teeth      fallen

                                                            He
                                              last of the Greeks!


[JS]

78

# FROM THE SOVEREIGN SUN (1971) ❦❦❦❦❦❦❦❦❦❦❦❦❦❦❦❦❦❦❦❦❦

## THE MAD MAD BOAT

A SONG

A ship decked with flags sails over the mountains
    and it starts manoeuvring: Heave-ho

It drops anchor among the pine trees
    it loads up with fresh air on both sides

It is made of black stone and of dream
    And it has an innocent boatswain and a cunning sailor

It comes out of the depths of old times
    It unloads sufferings and sighs

Christ, my Lord, I say it and I wonder
    at this mad mad boat this crazy ship

We've sailed on it for years and we haven't sunk yet
    One thousand captains we've changed

We were never afraid of cataclysms
    We entered everywhere and we went through everything

And we have on our mast an eternal
    sentinel, the Sun the Sovereign Sun!

[NV]

# FROM THE MONOGRAM

## (1971)

## SECTION VII

In Paradise I have marked out an island
You all over—and a house on the sea

With a large bed and a small door
And I have thrown into the unfathomable deep an echo
To mirror myself every morning when I wake up

To see you going by half immersed in the water
And to lament the other half of you in Paradise.


[NV]

# FROM THE LIGHT TREE AND THE FOURTEENTH BEAUTY (1971) ❦❦❦❦❦❦❦❦❦❦❦❦❦❦❦❦❦❦❦❦

## ON THE CITY

With four stones and a little sea water        I built a Temple and I sat there
to guard it

Noon came on suddenly and what we call thought pulsated in the black
grape to the breaking point

Something must be happening in the sky which can be touched by the
body like a wet dream

"Slowly        in the Hall great with echoes        the bearded one ap-
proached the cage and opened the little gate        So many centuries of toil
for a movement as small as the key-bearer's        that everyone wished to,
but did not dare, make

The curtains stirred and the bird's sound arrived even before its image
touching the roof

It shone around the sculptures and over the peristyle for a moment as still
as vertigo        where the trees were striking at the northern window and
you saw the radiance being displaced until

There she was      the naked woman      with the green halo around her hair and the little vest threaded with gold wires      she came and sat gently on the flagstones with half-open legs

A thing that in my perception took on the meaning of a flower when danger opens up its first tenderness      And later      exactly as

In the Book of Revelation      one after another the four horses rode by: the black one      the silver one      the guilty one      and the one that was dream-struck      without saddle or rider      in order to show that their glory had passed away

And look how the crowds march behind them      a whole army of people      they march on to be engulfed by the gehenna of Paradise      as it was written

Opposite her the man opened his robe      and his beautiful animal moved forward desiring a life in the land of forests and suns."

I smelled the body of a fig tree in the air      as it came towards me still fresh from the sea's paints

And I made movements over it until I woke up sweetly and I felt its milk sticking between my legs

Furiously I went on writing "On the City" utterly absorbed in the boundless grey

And in the transparent great leaves      At a given moment the islands appeared      and still higher in the aether all the ways in which the birds fly progressively into the infinite.

[NV]

## LITTLE GREEN SEA

Little green sea thirteen years old
Whom I would like to adopt
To send you to school in Ionia
That you may learn of the mandarin and the absinthe
Little green sea thirteen years old
On the small lighthouse tower at noon
You'll turn the sun over and you'll hear
How fate is undone and how
From hill to hill our distant
Relatives still communicate
They who hold up the air like a statue
Little green sea thirteen years old
With the white open collar and the ribbon
You'll enter from a window into Smyrna
To copy the gleam on the roof for me
Of the Kyrieleison and the Glory Be
With a little of the North Wind and the Levant
Wave after wave turning back
Little green sea thirteen years old
I'll sleep with you illegally
And I'll find deep in your arms
Pieces of stone with the words of the Gods
Pieces of stone with the fragments of Heracleitus.


[NV]

# THE FRESCO

Having loved and lived for centuries within the sea I learned to read and
write

So that now I can see     backwards to a great depth     the generations
one above the other     much as one mountain rises up before the other's
finished

And the same again in front:

The dark bottle     with the new Helen on the arm     her side against
the quicklime

Pouring the Holy Virgin's wine     half her body already fled to Asia
across the water

And the entire embroidery     displaced in the sky     with the swallow-
tailed birds     the yellow flowers     and the suns.


[JS]

## ARCHETYPE

The stricken pebble's gunpowder     reminded me of Ligoneri and a certain beach

On which I must have first seen Woman    and what it means    to see
the luminous rose trees of midnight    later I understood

When I found her to be a dove

When I found she was Sleep    clusters of waterdrops in her embrace

When I found her on a small balcony being dismantled by the gale

Till finally just a shoulder remained and the right part of her hair

Above the ruins    and the first Evenstar.


[JS]

## From THE LIGHT TREE

IV

No house remained now on the distant island     only when the south
wind blew you could see in its place a Monastery     extended above by
the clouds     while below the waterline     gurgling     the greenish
water licked the walls and the great iron gates

I paced about glowing with a red light     from ill-treatment and loneli-
ness

Entirely futile monks chanted and studied and no one let me in to see
again the places I grew up in     the places where my mother scolded
me     where the light tree first burgeoned and for whose sake     if it
should still exist

Somewhere the smoke was passing through     from Saint Isidore's
glance perhaps     the message came

That all our sufferings are deserved     and the order is not to be over-
thrown

Oh where can you be now my poor light tree     where are you light tree
    I raved as I ran     I need you now     now that I've lost even my
name

Now that no one mourns nightingales     and everyone writes poems.


[JS]

# PALINTROPE

Courage: This is the sky
And we are its birds
                    those which resemble no one

Sunk inside us
A sea of cereals with lands and extended cattle stalls

Lone outsider the sunflower

But who is he who walks in the sun
Black      as the light becomes stronger?

Courage: This being is
Kyon the dog as they call him
                                the almost *Archalcyon*

Pure open spaces of June nomad winds
Ploughed brown soils which we climbed

Thirsty for some light from Mount Tabor

But what is this which passes below and shudders
As if a little breeze had come from the other world?

Courage: This is death
Over the wide poppy
                        and over the tiny little camomile.

[NV]

## WHAT CANNOT COME ABOUT

I wish nostalgia had a body so that I could push it out of the win-
dow!     I want to shatter what cannot come about!     Girl from whose
naked breast     God once saved me as from a raft

And he led me high above the walls with the crescent moon just in case

You might appear on account of my own indiscretion     and the Fates
take aim at you     As indeed came about     Because such things are
what life wants and loves while we believe them to be elsewhere

And on the other side of love     and on the other side of death     we
sleepwalk until     the flesh of our flesh     tightens around us unbear-
ably     as the phosphorus inside us catches fire and lights up and we
awaken

Yes     time flows straight     but love is vertical and either they are cut
in two halves     or they never meet     Except what remains

As the sand borne by a strong wind in the rooms     and the spider and
outside on the threshold

The wolf with the round eye howling     everything seems likely     and
particularly the mountains of Crete which I kept in snow when I was little
and I found them again just as fresh     but what does this mean

Even if you remain free or victorious     the sun will set once more and
around you

There is a silence full of destroyed shores     where the clouds still come
down to graze     shortly before darkness falls forever

As if humanity had come to an end     and nothing timely remained to
be said.


[NV]


88

# AS LONG AS THE STAR LASTED

The watermelon froze my teeth and Helen
Remained half open as long as the star lasted

"That which you see is the weight of the mountain
Extracted from the scarf with the six Chimeras

The one you see there is the comet Felsfevor
Many years before its arrival and it still resembles Christ's

Face and the joy the wind makes before it fades away

That one with her hair shaped like a horn is called fever
Which will polish the children and may even take them away

And these the threads in the sand of peace

We will see more still
At one point Hermes Trismegistus will appear

Beneath the zincs with overcast skies and fluorine

Or perhaps the accordion might be heard
Black on black which cannot be explained."

And the star lasted as long as Helen looked
And the watermelon made the teeth freeze.


[NV]

## SILVER GIFT POEM

I know all this is nothing     and that the language I speak has no alphabet

Since even the sun and the waves are a syllabic script which can be deciphered only in times of exile and sorrow

And our country     a fresco covered by successive overlays Frankish or Slav     and should you try to restore it you are at once imprisoned and must render account

To a rabble of foreign Powers     always through the instrumentality of your own

As is the custom with disasters

And yet     let us imagine children playing     on an old threshing floor which could even be in a tenement     and that the loser

Must by the rules     speak and forfeit some truth to the others

So that at last they all find themselves holding in their hand a small

Silver gift poem.


[JS]

# FROM THE SIBLINGS
## (1977) 🌱🌱🌱🌱🌱🌱🌱🌱🌱🌱🌱🌱🌱🌱🌱🌱🌱🌱🌱

### PSALM AND MOSAIC
### FOR A SPRINGTIME IN ATHENS

Spring violet fragment
Spring down of a dove
Spring multicoloured dust

On the open books and papers
A warm little breeze was blowing
With gypsies it caught up
Like
Kites
In the air
And birds trying out their new rudders

Spring bitter lentisk
Spring vapour of the armpits
Spring invisible sesame

Along a wire that flashed  with fire
On a streetcorner with Caryatids
A tram
Screeched by
The sun in the empty terrain scraped with tongs
The nettles and the snail-marked grass

Spring antheap of the day
Spring blood of a bulb
Spring machinegun ripped loose

       In the hands of beautiful women
       Firing
       At random
       Death
       Millions of spermatozoids
       In the hands of beautiful women
       The strong flowers with sun inside them

Spring cheap cloth on pointed breasts
Spring hand landing like a wasp .
Spring "no"   "they'll see us"   "monster"

       And the monster wandered like a street organ
       In an unknown
       Strange
       Neighbourhood
       And the brutal clasp of the hand biding its time
       "Ah well, a throw must find its dice
       And a windowpane its daring stone!"

Spring crystal and nickel
Spring gardens that waver
Spring "Sing the Anger . . ."

       Oh Goddess! And how curly those dark places
       And those lips what sugar of violets
       And what a little garden
       The fresh
       Loose
       Hair
       What a journey on the soft breathing belly

Spring half-dizzy rain
Spring head of Zeus and the sea
Spring Mercury Air Sedan

The bells far out on the empty blueness
Under the eyelids opened a whirlpool
Swallowing
White
Down
And the hormones of a berry tree
Conquer the heights

Spring unbitten berry
Spring a kiss like a screw
Spring the gap of fainting

The beam wanted more nails
The ochres awaken the memory of a hospital
The song that glittered with gold scarabs
And circled
Low
In the courtyard with red and white tiles

Spring buzzing in the temples
Spring hammer and anvil
Spring sinking headfirst

Someone from the open window threw
Words that broke like almonds
Cactus
Castor
Condor
Falcon
While in the girls' school opposite

Spring 37 and 2
Spring Love Amour and Liebe
Spring No Nein and Non!

The girls bit the rubber erasers
And threw back their heads
As if
They drew out

The entrails
Of the sacrificed rooster
The pieces of entrails between their teeth

Spring angry tooth
Spring fuchsia of paroxysm
Spring an artesian volcano

    And other girls hidden behind the loft
    Fighting rose-coloured ribbon
    One minute
    Only
    The naked breasts
    The trembling shoots in the fields
    Where the locusts are merry

Spring jump of the heart
Spring dark womb
Spring unnameable act

    Over the open books and papers
    A violet
    Spot of light
    Came
    And went
    The spilt waters, the unclothed limbs
    Shining behind the shutter

Spring spring setting out for the open
Spring spring decked with flags
Spring "goodbye goodbye to you all!"


[NV]

94

# SMALL ANALOGUE

*For N. Hatzikyriakos Ghikas*

For just so long
As the surf needs to polish a pebble
Or the sky's chill at dawn to mark
The surface of a purple fig

There too
Far in Time's freezing depths
Where the black desert isle is lashed by the south wind

There too for just so long: the Invisible flourishes!

Yet we build and cultivate it
Yet we speak of it day and night

And often as he looks upon the holy and maternal land
Rising
From out of the continent's leprosy

We offer him again as in a dream
The stone the dew or the celestial mortar

O man of clay

See where night's birth pangs have brought forth
Cyan and cinnabar ochre and porphyry

Turn your sight high as acute thought
To cross the embattled firmament

And say we awkward ones are but

The tracks you followed, left
By the wild bee and the mourning sheep.


[JS]

# THE LEAF DIVINER

Tonight eighth of August
Shipwrecked on the shallows of the stars
My old house with the lizards
And the melted candle on the chest of drawers
Doors and windows open
My old house unloading
The burden of solitude in the night.

Startled voices and other ones which still
Run through the leafage lit up like
The firefly's secret passage
From the depths of a life turned upside down
Inside the cold white of the eyes
Where time stands still
And the moon with altered cheek

Desperately approaches mine;
A rustling dark, as from a lost
Love returning, they begin:
"Don't." And then again, "Don't." "My Baby."
"It was your destiny." "One day you'll remember it."
"Child, little child with the brown hair."
"I who love you." "Say always." "Always."

And as in the unquenchable blackness
Which opens in two, a garden
Extinguished and burnt out,
All your substance goes and flounders
So, out of the backwaters of the soul
A muddy wave rises whose bubbles
Are so many other old sunsets

Windows trembling in the hesperian light
A moment when you bypassed happiness
Like a song in which a girl goes to hide
Her eyes filled with tears for you
Of all the sacredness of an embrace and an oath

Nothing nothing was wasted
On this evening of the eighth of August

From the flora of the depths once more
This same endless shudder
One by one and all together makes the leaves rustle
Mononologuing in the aramaic of another world:
"Child, little child with the brown hair
You were destined to be lost here
In order to be saved far away."
"Destined to be lost here to be saved far away."

And suddenly, like what was before and after was revealed;
All the seas became walkable with flowers;
Alone, but not alone; as always;
As when I was young I advanced
With an empty place on my right
And from on high the star Vega followed me
The patron Saint of all my loves.


[NV]

# From VILLA NATACHA

I

I have something transparent and incomprehensible to say
Like a birdsong in time of war.

Here, in a corner where I sat
To smoke my first cigarette in freedom
Awkward in my happiness, afraid
I might break a flower, or hurt a bird
And so put God in a difficult position

Yet everything obeys me
The upright cane-brakes and the leaning belfry
And the whole firmament of the garden
Mirrored in my mind
One by one the names echo
Strangely in the foreign language: Phlox, Aster, Cytise
Eglantine, Pervenche, Colchique
Alise, Frésia, Pivoine, Myoporone
Muguet, Bleuet
Saxifrage
Iris, Clochette, Myosotis
Primevère, Aubépine, Tubereuse
Paquerette, Ancolie, and all their shapes
Clearly outlined in the fruit: the circle, the square
The triangle and the rhombus
As the birds see them, to make the world simple
A drawing by Picasso
With woman, child and hippocentaur.

And I say: this too will come about, and that too will pass.
The world doesn't need much. A little
Something. Like the wrong turn of the rudder before an accident
Yet
Exactly

Towards
The opposite direction

Enough of this cult of danger—time now for a retribution on its part.

*I dream of a revolution against evil and wars like the one Matisse made against chiaroscuro and tones.*

[NV]

FROM MARIA NEFELI
(1979) ❦❦❦❦❦❦❦❦❦❦❦❦❦❦❦❦❦❦❦

TRANSLATED BY
Nanos Valaoritis

Maria Nefeli* says:

## THE CLOUD

*I live from day to day—who knows what tomorrow will bring.*
*My one hand crumples up the money and the other smoothes it out*

*You see weapons must speak in our chaotic times*
*and we must align ourselves with our so-called "national ideals"*

*Why are you staring at me, you scribbler—you who never wore a*
*    soldier's uniform*
*the art of making money is one of the martial arts also*

*Go stay up all night—writing thousands of bitter verses*
*go fill up the walls with revolutionary slogans*

*The others will always see you as an intellectual*
*and only I who love you: in my dreams I see you as a prisoner.*

*Therefore, if love is truly "a common divider," as they say,*
*I must be Maria Nefeli and you, alas, the Cloudgatherer.*

*Inscribe yourself somewhere as well as you can and*
*then again generously erase yourself.*

* *Nefeli* means "Cloud"

And the Other Speaker:

## THE CLOUDGATHERER

Ah how nice to be a cloudgatherer
to write epics on your old shoes as Homer did
not to care a bit if you please or not
zero

Unperturbed you reap unpopularity
this way; with generosity; as if you owned
a mint that you could close down
firing all the personnel
in order to cultivate a poverty all your own
that no one else possesses.
At this hour when thick-skinned people in their offices
desperately glued to their phones
struggle in vain
you rise inside Love
all soiled yet agile like a chimney-sweep
then climb down from Love ready to inaugurate
a white beach of your own

without money

you undress as those who pay attention to the stars undress
and with wide strokes you swim out in order to weep freely . . .

*It is bigamy both to love and to dream.*

Maria Nefeli says:

## DISCOURSE ON BEAUTY

*Be afraid,*
> *if you want the instinct of Beauty to wake up;*

*or if not, since we live in the century of photography,*
*make it stand still: that which stirs continually*
*next to us with strange gestures:*
> > *the Inconceivable!*

*a)  two beautiful hands of a woman (or even a man) that have become*
*familiar with wild pigeons*
*b)  a wire whose memories are all made of electric current and*
*unsuspecting birds*
*c)  a shout that might be said to be eternally relevant*
*d)  the paradox of the open sea.*

*You will of course have understood what I mean.*

*We are the negative of the dream:*
*that is why we seem black and white*
*and we experience decay*
*over a minimal reality. Yet*
*Das Reine, Ladies and Gentlemen,*
*kann sich nur darstellen im Unreinen*
*und versuchst du das Edle zu geben*
*ohne Gemeines*
*so wird es als das Allerunnatürlichste*
*says He who happened to cross*
*the High Paths.*

*And he must have known something.*


*My God, how much blue you spend to stop us from*
*seeing you!*

And the Other Speaker:

## THE DROP OF WATER

My lips burn and sorrow shines
a drop of clean water over the dark chasms
filled with grass; only the soul
lit up like an old church
                    shows that we will die in the spring . . .

Ding-ding the camomile; I'm weary of hoping
ding-ding the flower of mallow; I'm tired of worrying
ding-ding: such from the beginning
was man
            and I didn't even know it!

Those footsteps on the dry leaves
the lowing of Time's ox

the Pelasgian wall building along the whole length of my life
and myself walking beside it
until the black sea appears
and over it my three stars lighting up like fireworks!

Everything is a drop
of beauty trembling on the eyelashes:
a sorrow transparent like Mount Athos hanging from the sky
with infinite visibility
where all things are done and undone
Charon kneels and rises stronger
and falls back helpless sinking in the chasms.

The lone drop of water vigorous over the chasms.


*In the village of my language Sorrow is called The*
*    Shiner.*

Maria Nefeli says:

## THE TROJAN WAR

*If only we lived upside down*
*would we see everything right side up? Hmph. The upside down*
*has a stubborn permanence;*
*it is, as they say, the rule.*
*Which means that if we succeed in living*
*we certainly live by exceptions.*
*We make believe that nothing is happening*
*precisely in order that something might occur*
*apart and above the mockery.*
*A cherry, when inside it*
*all the miseries are wintering*
*and in spite of them it shines,*
*clean and mighty and impeccable, showing*
*what could have been the superiority of the human being.*

*The drop of blood every April*
*free for everyone.*

*Unhappy scouts upside down*
*drivers of heavy tanks on the sky*
*even the clouds are mined*
*beware: spring depends on us.*

*Let's give the soil back to our feet.*
*Greenery to greenery, Neanderthal man*
*to Neanderthal man. Muscles are useless*
*what's needed is monstrous love*
*what's needed is a tigress's leap into ideas.*
*As long as Achaeans exist there will be Helen of Troy*
*even if the hand is not where the neck is*

*Every age has its Trojan War.*

*Far away*
        *in the furthermost depths of the Lamb*
                *the war continues.*

And the Other Speaker:

HELEN

Maria Nefeli no doubt
is a sharp girl
a real threat to the future
sometimes she glitters like a knife
with a drop of blood on her
she has the same meaning
that the Lambda of the Iliad once had.

Maria Nefeli marches forward
liberated from the horrible notion of the eternal cycle.

With her mere existence
she finishes off half the human race.

Maria Nefeli lives in the antipodes of Morality
yet she is entirely ethical.

When she says "I'll sleep with this one"
she means that she will once more kill History.
You should have seen then what enthusiasm seizes the birds.

Anyway with her manner
she eternalizes the nature of the olive tree.
She becomes, depending on the moment,
sometimes silvery and sometimes deep blue.

That is why the rivals continually
go off on military campaigns—look:
others with their social theories
many just waving flowers

Every age has its Helen.


*From your reflection the sun becomes solid in*
*the pomegranate*
*and feels good.*

The Other Speaker says:

## HYMN IN TWO DIMENSIONS

Now I love you in two dimensions

like an Etruscan figure
like a sign from Klee that was once a fish
you advance dodecaphonic
enervating
in a flash
beautiful
with waves of the Caribbean in your pleated skirt
with heavy blue beads from Pandrosou Street
around your neck.

Face watery idol
arriving like the light
of a star which vanished
centuries ago.

Then I listen to the waters and I understand you.
Even if you haven't any idea about it
(the Signaller is never aware of his mission)
and I observe behind the paleness of the makeup
the endless road I followed
to be able to speak to you in this manner

Voie lactée ô soeur lumineuse

The only destiny I didn't choose
My God—that very one I took upon me.

*In the unjust distribution*

          *God always comes out worse.*

And Maria Nefeli says:

## OFFICIAL DECLARATION

*Observe very closely the frag-*
*mentation of my daily life*
*and its ostensible inconsequence*
*its direction*
*and its ultimate aims*
*its attempts to develop*
*to acquire a deeper meaning.*
*She seems to discourage the research of scientists*
*in favour of—I believe—the authenticity of man.*

*On this*
            *en las purpureas horas*
*I make no concessions.*

*It is impossible for me to see myself*
*differently*
*except as an anti-narrative composition*
*without historical conscience*
*without a deep probe of a psychological kind*
*something which would make my daily life*
*boring as a novel*
*ephemeral like a movie*
*negative as a joke*
*indifferent like a painting of the Renaissance*
*harmful like a political action generally*
*slavish and submissive to the natural order of the world*
*and—as is commonly said—to feelings of philanthropy.*

*A law code*
*totally useless for the Authorities*
                        *would be a real blessing.*

Maria Nefeli says:

## THE POETS

*What can I do my dears with you Poets*
*for years you have been impersonating invincible souls*

*And for years you expected what I didn't expect*
*standing in line like unwanted objects . . .*

*If they call upon you—none of you answers*
*outside all hell has broken loose and everything is on fire*

*But you, you claim imperviously—I'd like to know with what in mind—*
*your rights over the void!*

*Now at a time when wealth is a cult oh with what insouciance*
*you exude the vanity of ownership*

*You walk on holding the unfortunate black-clad*
*Globe wrapped up in Palm Sunday's leaves*

*And among the fumes of human sulphuric acid*
*you become the willing guinea pigs of the Sacred.*

*Man is attracted to God*

*as the shark to blood.*

And the Other Speaker:

## THAT WHICH CONVINCES

Please pay attention to my lips: the world depends on them.
On the connections they risk and on their unacceptable
comparisons, as when some evening that smells good
we trip over the Moon's woodcutter and make him fall down
and he bribes us with some jasmine and we consent . . .

That which convinces I believe resembles the chemical substance which
    suffers change.
Although the cheek of a girl may be beautiful
all of us with decayed faces will return one day from the Land of Truth.

Friends, I don't know how to make it clear to you
but we have to be substituted for the old Robbers.
Let's send our hand to reach
there where a woman like an Apple Tree waits half hidden in the clouds
totally ignoring the distance that separates us.

And something more: when it begins to rain
let's strip and shine like the clover leaf . . .

*A sea which is a mistake is impossible.*

# NOTE ON
# ODYSSEUS ELYTIS

ODYSSEUS ELYTIS was born in Crete in 1911 into a well-known industrial family that originally came from Lesbos. The family moved to Athens in 1914, and Elytis has maintained a residence there since. He was educated in Athenian secondary schools and at the University of Athens, where he studied law but did not take a degree. In 1935 he published his first poems in *Ta Nea Grammata* (The New Letters), the periodical that became the principal outlet for the so-called "Generation of the Thirties," which included George Seferis, Andreas Embirikos and several other poets who, along with Elytis, were responsible for introducing French surrealism into Greek poetry. Elytis also began to create collages at this time, an interest that reasserted itself some thirty years later, under the 1967–1974 dictatorship. In 1940–1941, the poet served as a Second Lieutenant in the First Army Corps during the Albanian Campaign against the invading Italian forces. During the post-war years, Elytis devoted himself almost exclusively to his writing, with two brief periods of public service as Director of Programming for the National Broadcasting Institute of Athens and a term as President of the Governing Board of the Greek Ballet. In 1960 his *The Axion Esti* was awarded the National Prize for Poetry, and he was subsequently decorated with the Order of the Phoenix. From 1948 to 1952, and again from 1969 to 1971, he lived in France. In the early 1960s he visited both the United States and Russia, and since receiving the Nobel Prize in 1979 he has travelled extensively in Europe.

# NOTES ON THE
# TRANSLATORS

EDMUND KEELEY is Professor of English and Creative Writing at Princeton University. He has translated the complete poems of Cavafy and Seferis and a selection of Sikelianos in collaboration with Philip Sherrard. His translation of Yannis Ritsos's poems, *Ritsos in Parentheses*, received the Landon Translation Award from the Academy of American Poets. He is the author of four novels and a critical study, *Cavafy's Alexandria*.

PHILIP SHERRARD has taught at St. Anthony's College, Oxford, and King's College, London, and now lives in Greece. In addition to the translations of Greek poetry in which he has collaborated with Edmund Keeley, he has published two books on modern Greek literary themes, *The Marble Threshing Floor* and *The Wound of Greece*. His collections of poetry are *Orientation and Descent* and *Motets for a Sunflower*. He is currently co-editor of the review *Temenos*.

GEORGE SAVIDIS is Professor of Modern Greek at the University of Salonika and George Seferis Visiting Professor of Modern Greek Studies at Harvard University. He is the editor of the Greek texts of Cavafy, Seferis and Sikelianos, among others, and with Edmund Keeley he has translated a selection of Cavafy's "unpublished" poems, *Passions and Ancient Days*, as well as Elytis's *The Axion Esti*.

JOHN STATHATOS is a Greek-born poet, photographer and journalist who now lives in London, where he runs Oxus Press. He has translated Takis Sinopoulos's *Selected Poems* and work by several of the younger Greek poets, including Nassos Vayenas's *Biography and Other Poems*. His most recent collection of poems is *In Passage*.

NANOS VALAORITIS is a Greek poet and critic who is Professor of Comparative Literature and Writing at San Francisco State University. In the 1940s he introduced modern Greek poetry to British readers through articles in *Horizon*, translations of Elytis's poems in *Daylight*, *New Writing*, and *Orpheus*, edited by John Lehmann, and the first translation of Seferis's selected poems, *The King of Asine and Other Poems* (with Bernard Spencer and Lawrence Durrell, 1948). He has published several collections of poetry and of prose in both Greek and English.